Ava Meets Amigo, the Teardrop

A Story and Activity Book About Dealing With Grief and Loss

Betts H. Gatewood, Ed.S., LPC

Edited by Susan Bowman
Layout and design by Tonya Daugherty

ISBN—1889636843

Library of Congress Control Number:
2005921022

10 9 8 7 6 5 4 3 2 1
Printed in the United States

PO Box 115 • Chapin, SC 29036
(800) 209-9774 • (803) 345-1070 • Fax (803) 345-0888
yl@sc.rr.com • www.youthlightbooks.com

Dedication

To our darling Ava,

our precious grandchild,

truly a gift from God

Acknowledgements

Thank you to all the children who have shared their feelings

with me over the years. Together we have learned the power

of expressing feelings through words, drawings, laughter, and

tears. I hope that Amigo can be a personal friend to all of you

as you continue your life's journeys.

6

Introduction

Ava Meets Amigo is a story for a caring adult and child to read together to help the child explore the feeling of grief and learn coping skills. Amigo, a friendly teardrop, finds Ava sad due to a favorite aunt's illness. Amigo helps Ava understand that teardrops are our friends. He also shows her many things she can do to help herself feel better during this time of worry and uncertainty.

The story pages are faced with pages that contain discussion questions the reader can ask as he and the child are reading together. These questions will help a child personalize the feelings Ava is having, and bring her closer to understanding how the story fits her life and situation.

The adult could read the story through the first time without using the questions, then reread it adding the discussion suggestions. Children love to hear stories more than once, and this gives them the opportunity to experience it before having to think about their answers.

This book also includes activity pages at the end. These can be used to extend the learning and understanding of this universal feeling, sadness, which can sometimes also be a terrifying one for a child.

Discussion Questions

- Do you ever cry when you are sad?

- What do you think is making Ava sad?

- Who do you think is talking to Ava?

Ava was feeling sad. She was trying to be a "big girl" and not cry, but it was very hard. When she got to her room, she realized that a tear had just popped up in the corner of her eye. As she was reaching up to wipe it away she heard, "Now wait a minute. I may be of some help to you. Don't wipe me away just yet." Surprised, Ava looked around to see who was talking to her.

Discussion Questions

• How do you think Ava felt when a teardrop started talking to her?

• How would you feel?

• What do you think the teardrop will say to Ava? How can he make her feel better?

10

It was a teardrop! How could a teardrop help her to feel better? But since she was lonely, she decided to see what he had to say.

She asked him, "Who are you, and how can you help me feel better?"

11

Discussion Questions

- What language is "Amigo"? What does "amigo" mean in English?

- Amigo says it is OK to cry sometimes. What do you think?

- How can teardrops be our friends?

12

"My name is Amigo, and as you can see I am a teardrop. I understand how it feels to be sad, and I would like to be your friend. Sometimes people forget that I can be a friend. They think that teardrops are not supposed to be seen. They think that everyone is supposed to look and feel happy all the time."

"Well, I'm not happy today," said Ava. "I would rather be happy cause that's more fun, but I just can't be happy today."

13

Discussion Questions

- What are some reasons why people get sick?

- Have you ever known someone who is sick that you worried about?

- What are some other things that might make a child sad?

14

Amigo told her, "Sad things happen to everyone, and to all ages, even children. Has something sad happened to you?"

"Yes," said Ava sadly. "My aunt is very sick and I heard someone say she is in the hospital. I'm scared about what may happen to her. Maybe if I had been quieter when I played at her house she would not be so sick."

15

Discussion Questions

- Amigo says it is ok to feel sad sometimes. What other feelings are ok for children to have?

- What things make you feel sad like Ava?

- What might make her feel better?

"Oh, Ava," said Amigo. "You are not the reason she is sick. She is sick because something is wrong with her body. This happens sometimes to people, and it is not your fault. Sometimes medicine and doctors can make people feel better and sometimes they cannot. It is OK to feel sad when someone you love is sick."

"But how can I make myself feel better, Amigo? I don't like feeling sad."

Discussion Questions

- What do you think Ava is doing right now that will make her feel better?

- What are some sad things that might happen to adults?

- Have you ever seen an adult cry? If you have, how does that make you feel? Were you surprised? Is that all right for an adult to cry?

18

"Well, Ava," Amigo answered, "being sad isn't a bad thing. It's how all of us, even adults, feel when something happens we don't like. But there are things we can do to help ourselves feel better, and you are doing one of them right now."

"I am?"
Ava
asked.

Discussion Questions

- Did you know that talking to someone can make you feel better?

- Who are some people you can talk to when you are sad?

- How do you feel after you have talked to someone about your feelings?

"Yes, you are, answered Amigo. You are talking about your feelings to someone, and saying how you feel about what is happening. There are lots of people you can talk to besides me, your new friend, Amigo. You can talk to your parents, grandparents, caregiver, teacher, counselor, or minister."

Discussion Questions

- What could Ava write in her journal today about how she is feeling?

- How have Ava's feelings changed since she started talking to Amigo?

- Tell about a time when your feelings changed.

"What else can I do, Amigo?"

"You can write your feelings down in a
journal each day, and you will notice
that even though you are sad
some days are better
than others, and
your feelings
change."

Discussion Questions

- What kinds of fun times do you think Ava might have had with her aunt?

- What are some fun times you have had with your relatives?

- How do you feel when you remember a fun time you have had?

"I like to draw. Would drawing help too?"

"Yes, that's a great idea. You could draw
a picture of a good time you had with your
aunt, and send it to her with a short
note. That would make her feel
better I'm sure, and you would
both enjoy remembering
a fun time."

Discussion Questions

- What are some activities we can do even when we are feeling sad?

- Can you name anyone who feels happy all the time? Who?

- How does playing and doing our work make us feel better?

Ava thought of something else. "I have some pictures of me and my aunt I could look at too. She liked to send me pictures when we did fun things together."

Amigo saw that Ava was feeling a little better and he added another idea. "You can also keep playing, laughing, doing your schoolwork, and being a good friend to others. Your aunt would want you to keep being a happy little girl even though you are worried about her and feeling sad sometimes."

Discussion Questions

- Ava likes to do lots of things outdoors. What kinds of activities do you like to do outside?

- How can these activities help us feel better?

- Who are some special people you like to do these activities with?

Ava added, "I love reading and taking walks with my parents. Is it ok to keep doing that even though my aunt is sick?"

Amigo said, "of course. And you can ride your bike, play games with your friends, and do other things you like to do."

29

Discussion Questions

- How do you feel inside after you have cried a little while?

- What do Amigo, and other teardrops, want to do for Ava?

- How can a teardrop be your friend, like Amigo is for Ava?

"And there's one more thing, Ava. Don't forget me, your friend Amigo the teardrop. You can cry! Cry with someone else or cry alone. We teardrops are your friends and can help you feel better. It is OK to cry when you are sad."

Discussion Questions

- How is Ava feeling now? What made her feel better?

- When we are sad one day does that mean we will be sad all the time?

- What are some ways you can think of to take good care of yourself when you are sad?

Ava took a deep breath, cried a few more tears, then went to her art table to get some paper and crayons to make a special picture for her aunt. Amigo watched as she worked, and knew that she was learning how to take good care of herself and her feelings. This would help her feel better soon.

33

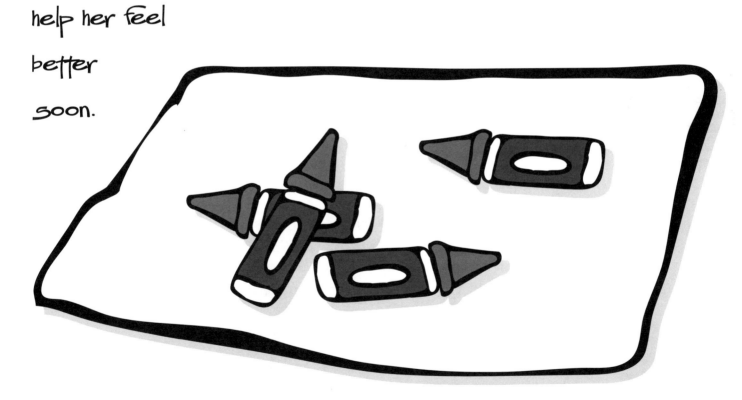

Discussion Questions

- Have you ever seen someone cry when they were happy? Have you ever cried when you were happy?

- How can you tell that Ava and Amigo are good friends now?

- How about you, do you think you could be friends with your teardrops?

Ava held up her picture for Amigo to see. She had drawn her aunt playing in the ocean and jumping waves with her. As Amigo and Ava looked at the picture they started laughing together. Ava said, "I didn't know teardrops laughed too." Amigo told her, "Sure, sometimes people even cry when they are happy. I told you we were your friends."

Ava smiled at him, and knew that she would remember all Amigo had told her, and let him help her feel better any time she was sad.

Activity Pages

Draw a picture of Amigo and Ava doing something fun outside together.

37

What are some things you could do to make yourself feel better when you are sad? Amigo has gotten you started by listing 5 ideas, now you add to the list!

1. Ride bicycle

2. Help Mom or Dad do a chore.

3. Call a friend to come play.

4. Read a book.

5. Listen to a favorite tape or CD.

6. _____

7. _____

8. _____

9. _____

10. _____

38

Write a creative story pretending you are Amigo and you are trying to help a child whose puppy has died. What would you say? How could you help her?

_____

_____

_____

_____

_____

_____

_____

_____

_____

39

Pretend you are writing in Ava's journal about her aunt, or someone you know who is very sick. Your journal entry could start like this:

and I have had lots of fun times together. We

Amigo is the Spanish word for "friend." Match the following words for "friend" with the language they are from:

Amigo	English
Ami	German
Friend	Dutch
Freund	French
Amico	Spanish
Vriend	Italian

41

For younger children:

Connect the dots to see who can help us feel better when we are sad.

42

For younger children:

Color Amigo a color that you like.

43

About the Author

Betts H. Gatewood, Ed.S., LPC, is an elementary school counselor, with 25 years experience in elementary and middle school counseling. Betts has led numerous workshops and training sessions for faculties, counselors, and parents and presented nationally at counseling conventions. She and her husband, Art, are the proud parents of three adult children and one granddaughter and reside in Fort Mill, SC.

44